A *Victim*

Or

A *Victor*

A VICTIM OR A VICTOR

Copyright © Cynthia Shaw
ISBN: 978-1-958186-02-2
LOC: 2022909305

Publisher, Editor and Book Design: Fiery Beacon Publishing House, LLC
Fiery Beacon Consulting and Publishing Group

Graphics: FBPH Graphics Team, Dashona Smith

This work was produced in Greensboro, North Carolina, United States of America. All rights reserved under International Copyright Law.

A *Victim*

Or

A *Victor*

Cynthia Shaw

Table of Contents

This book is in loving memory of my husband of forty-two ½ years. I love you so much, but God loved you more. You are truly missed. I find comfort in dedicating this book in your honor.

Pearlee Shaw, Jr.

August 17, 1955 – October 20, 2018

To my children, grandchildren, spiritual children. Thank you for pushing me to write this book. May the life I live speak for me. Continue to live for God. Nothing else matters when God is in control.

I love you!

Mom, Grandma, Fancy Grancy and Momma Shaw

A Beautiful Flower

As a flower grows stronger and beautiful each day.

There comes a time when they too must go away.

You stood strong while on earth even though in pain your faith remained.

You were the beautiful rose in the center of us all, praying and pushing us to trust God and always stand tall.

This book is dedicated to the beautiful flower that help me to grow. Cassandra Elliott you will always be one of my angels watching over me. Sing on my beautiful flower!

Pastor Cassandra Elliott

March 10, 1968 – June 27, 2021

The Foreword

"Love shows up!"

-Pastor Cassandra Elliott

Life is filled with many twists and turns, and oftentimes, the probability of survival seems bleak, even in the face of those who know you. If we are not careful, we can find ourselves in a place of almost agreeing with what is trying to take us out personally, spiritually, emotionally and more. In spite of this attempt there is a remnant, there is a people, who have the capacity to survive the hard places and obtain undeniable victory.

I will never forget the day that I met Author Cynthia Shaw, AKA, "Momma Shaw." For more months than I can count, my mentor, Pastor Cassandra Elliott kept telling me about her, how much she loved her and how much of a jewel she was. From the moment we met, the power of God on her life could not be ignored. I called her then, and even more now, a "quiet power," a vessel who has fully surrendered to God, and who He knows He can freely use for His glory! So here we are, being brought to the crossroads of being one of two things, a victim or a victor. The answer to this question cannot be compromised or accepted with conditions; instead, it must be fully viewed and fully decided without regret.

The Word of God tells us that we do not have a choice to follow the middle ground or have it the way we want it, also known as, the "have your cake and eat it, too," syndrome. Instead, we are eventually faced with the mandate of choice – a choice driven, in partiality, by what we have gone through while ultimately led by the spirit dwelling inside of us. The process and qualifiers are different for different people, and if I can be honest, though it's a different road, that does not mean that it won't lead us to the same place. For Author Shaw, the crossroads came in the form of not realizing her destiny (at first), going through the process as a caregiver for her husband, making it to forty-two and ½ years of purposed marriage and later losing him to a disease called cancer. Despite the obstacles, here she still stands, stronger now than she was back then. For you, it may be something against your house, your family, or your church, but nevertheless, the crossroad is necessary.

As you prepare to dive in, remember, there are no split decisions here. This book will bring you into the world of Author Shaw, but also forcefully but strongly push you in the direction of RECOVERY. As I learned at my job, "BE PRESENT NOW!" In other words, do not allow anything to take your focus and vision away from this deciding moment. Decide NOW that you are going to focus, prepare, make accommodations for the overflow that God sends in response to this literary work. I know I speak for the great author of this vision when I say.....

The portal is open, so push.

We can't wait to see what God births out of you!

Prophet Brandi L. Rojas, **C.E.O.**

Fiery Beacon Publishing House, LLC

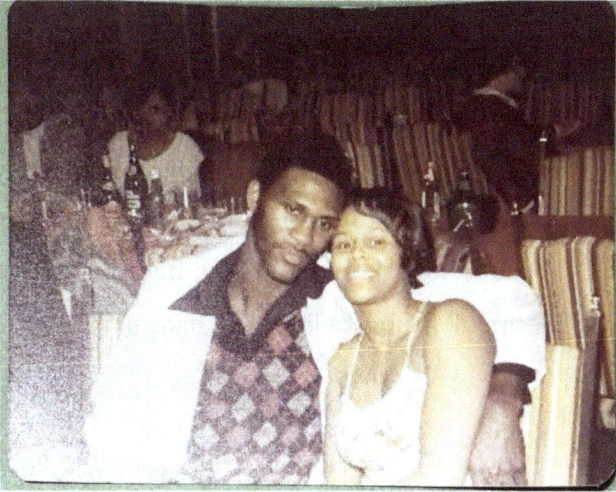

⁴ Love suffers long *and* is kind; love does not envy; love does not parade itself, is not ᴸᴸpuffed up; ⁵ does not behave rudely, does not seek its own, is not provoked, ᴸᴸthinks no evil; ⁶ does not rejoice in iniquity, but rejoices in the truth; ⁷ bears all things, believes all things, hopes all things, endures all things.

⁸ Love never fails.

1 Corinthians 13:4-8 (AMP)

The Introduction

Every love story has its humble beginnings, so allow me a few moments to share with you about mine, an unconditional love.

When I was seven years old, this young man (boy) came to me saying that he was going to marry me. Without a moment of hesitation, I told him NO! (not my exact words). We grew up in the same neighborhood and went to the same school together, so for us to meet simply "made sense." We were friends but never more than that, at least in my view. One would think that after I said no the first time, he would have let the whole idea go, but that was not the case at all. Once we became teenagers, I guess he figured that my answer could not last forever, so he took a chance and asked me again. I finally said "YES" but that decision only lasted for one day. Now, let me be clear, I was excited about the idea of him being my "man," but he was arrogant, and I wasted no time telling him so! This attitude did not just create itself, he was a great athlete, and he knew it; no one could take that truth from him.

Despite anyone who may have been thrilled at the thought of us finally being together, I couldn't see it because it wasn't God's timing yet. As all teenagers do eventually, we split ways after graduation. He ended up going to college (High Point University). While he was gone, I began doing my own thing but desired to find that special one (the young people today would call it finding "my person.") After realizing that my way was not the best way and that my arms were too short to box with God, I finally stopped looking and prayed. On three occasions, I dreamed of being at a basketball game watching this young man playing ball. I did not understand the dream because I wasn't dating anyone, nor was I going to any games. (Ladies despise not your Naomi blessing.) Even though the young man that courted me in high school was a star basketball player, remember, I had already kicked him out of my heart and mind, so my dream involving him never became a thought in my mind.

I will never forget this, the day that his mom tried to set us up, "not down but up," and invited me to one of his games. I had not seen him play since high school, so the invite did not make much sense to me, but I accepted. He was now getting ready to go into his junior year and despite what I felt was the best he could ever be in our "growing up" years, he had become an even better basketball player! He was shooting three-pointers before they started counting them in the game. They won that night and went on to the finals the next night but lost the championship game by a last second shot that was ruled after the buzzer.

We went on a date that night and then breakfast the next morning only to talk about what each other was doing in life, oh, and to listen to him talk about his girlfriends. I don't know if it was the breakfast or the conversation, but at some point, it clicked, that all of the dreams I had been so confused about was locked in the eyes of this young man who sat before me. The rest of our dating path went by in a flash. We dated less than one year before getting married.

The rest is history.

He gave up running in the Junior Olympics to marry me, his childhood love. We had two beautiful daughters that he loved with his whole heart. He believed strongly that the man is to provide for his family and did all that he could to do just that and more. He treated us like Queens, pure royalty, so much so, that some days I wanted to pinch myself to make sure that I was not dreaming.

Despite the fairy tale we lived in, I would be remiss if I did not tell you that there were bumps in the road; to tell you this story and say we didn't go through some things would be a lie. Nevertheless, we decided obedience was better than the sacrifice and so, we decided to fight through it. Have we been saved our whole lives? NO, but there comes a time in life when you must decide whose side you are on and as you can see, we chose the Lord's Side. Life can be tough and challenge our decision, even when the decision is the right one. This fight can even cause us to talk ourselves out of what God has ordained just for us. It amazes me how life can hit, and before we know it, we have attached our words to God's voice, only to realize later that our "exit strategy" is not God at all but our own disobedience. We have all been guilty of giving the devil too much of our time and our will, too.

We had financial troubles…But God

Sickness…But God

Health…But God

Good times and Bad times…But God

Why do we play the blame game? Why is it, that when things do not go our way, we blame everyone else but ourselves? Our God can do whatever He wants to do; when and how He wants to and if we have a true relationship with God, we will always surrender to His will.

After a three-year battle with cancer, my husband of forty-two ½ years died. My first thought was to blame myself — maybe it was something I didn't do right or something I failed to recognize. I could have easily blamed God for not giving him the extra fifteen years that he asked for and truthfully, my flesh wanted to. Why my husband? I could have asked. Why Not? My husband had gone to the cancer center every other week; sometimes he went two and three times a week for three years. Despite the illness, he remained to be the provider he had always been. He kept going to work every day, even after chemo treatments and when it got to be too much on his feet, he went to a foot doctor for some relief so that he could keep going. He took his role as king of his castle, and he provided for his family. I worked too, but he always said my money was "like the icing on the cake." For three years, I watched this man put his heart and soul into making sure his family would be okay and he was determined to prove that nothing would stop him from doing that, not even cancer.

In April 2016, he was told he was cancer-free; he was mis-diagnosed twice. He was then told that another mass had been found. As time progressed, it began to take a toll on his body. His health began to decline, especially after they gave him chemo and radiation in the same day. These treatments began to impact his everyday life; even to the point of not being able to write. Despite the trial, God restored his health again, and he went back to work but was very short-lived.

In September of 2018, he had to go into surgery. It was only supposed to be an overnight stay, but instead we spent the whole month of September in the hospital, twenty-three days to be exact. During this time, my husband only talked about life and living; not once did he say anything about death. My husband loved God, but I felt in my heart that he knew he was dying but wanted to be strong for me. He continued to show me love until that final day. That day he said NO to me and YES to God.

Did I become a victim or victor?

I could have felt like a victim and cried "If you had been here my husband wouldn't have died," but NO! God was right there the whole time, taking care of my husband and giving me the strength to be strong and face each day.

Lazarus – Will you respond in Worship?

Since his passing, I have learned to take life one day at a time, knowing that one day we will meet again. I had some great years with my husband.

Husbands love your wives as Christ loves the church. Treat her special whenever and as often as you can. Wives love your husbands. Show love and respect for each other. Single men and ladies allow God to put that special one in your life. It's not about making a list and checking it twice, three times or more but it is about God providing His very best for you and learning to build with one another. All things will work out if God is in it. There may be heartache and pain but know that we serve a God that sits high and looks low; there is nothing too hard for God! I miss my husband, that is an understatement and there have been some tears, but one thing I know for sure is, to be absent from the body is to be present with the Lord. Sleep in Heavenly peace my love, we shall meet again.

I have heard the Bible being read my whole life. It was not until I begin to read it for myself that I saw how my life was pattern after characters in the Bible. I begin to see God's Word come alive in my life like never before. As you begin to read through the pages of my book, I begin with references and character studies from the Bible. Am I putting myself as great as these characters — No! I just began to see how God took ordinary people to get the work He needed done, finished, and completed. You say, "I'm ordinary," but God says we are chosen people, a royal priesthood, a holy nation, and God's special possession. My prayer is that you see and hear my heart in each page, choosing to be victorious in life and not a victim. Are you going to remain a victim, or will you begin to walk in victory as a victor?

Had I chosen to be a victim, my life wouldn't have made me victorious. We go through life always thinking the grass is greener on the other side and that what you have gone through is worse than others, but that is so far from the truth. Whatever you have gone through, are going through or will go through, it has already been conquered through the blood of Jesus.

We have one life to live.

Let us live it to the fullness of God for His glory!

I used to look on others' lives and think that because they had money, fancy cars, clothes, etc. their lives were better than mine. God allowed me to see that what I had was so much greater. Not taking away from the people with those things but think about it! If you have those things and don't have love, peace, joy, and happiness, what good is it? They are just things. Who is the richer? I would rather have Jesus than silver and gold.

I AM A VICTOR!

I REFUSE TO BE ANYTHING LESS!

**As we prepare to take this journey together, use this
space to share one time in your life that you denied
destiny? When did you realize it? How did you recover it
or recover FROM it?**

_____

_____

_____

_____

_____

_____

_____

_____

_____

_____

_____

_____

_____

_____

_____

_____

_____

_____

_____

rades 3 and 4

HTS AND DESIRABLE DEEDS SUPPLY CONTINUED
GROWING NEEDS

Robert Warren. THIRD ROW: Arthur Williamson, Joanne Miles, James Hooker, Fred Connor, James Robinson, Larry Young, David Fuller, Ruthie Fuller, Robert Scales. NOT PICTURED: Harold Smith, Beverly Davis, Linda Dick, Pearlee Shaw, Frank Davis, and William Davis.

OFFICERS

Chapter 1:

Butterfly (Metamorphosis)

Life can take us though some rough and ugly stages, but do we stop because of the stages? Some of us do, thinking that stopping will at least cause the pain and the attack to subside, but what about the victory that is awaiting us? What about the answered prayer that stands waiting on the other side of our press? It is through life experiences that I have learned to accept the life of a butterfly for my life.

There are four stages of a butterfly's evolution:

1. Egg

2. Larva

3. Pupa (Chrysalis), and

4. Adult

Before our parents came together, He knew us. The Word of God shares this with us in *Jeremiah 1:5,*

"Before I formed you in the womb, I knew you [and approved of you as My chosen instrument], And before

you were born I consecrated you [to Myself as My own];
I have appointed you as a prophet to the nations."

The egg stage is a symbol of a new life beginning and is transformed into reality as our bodies began to form and came together. We are not created by accident or haphazardly, but instead are created specifically by God's design and blueprint.

For You formed my innermost parts; You knit me
[together] in my mother's womb. I will give
thanks *and* praise to You, for I am fearfully and
wonderfully made; Wonderful are Your works, And my
soul knows it very well.

Psalm 139:13

What an amazing God we serve! One who has invested time and effort into us without a doubt in His mind. Every time we take a breath, we are displaying God's masterpiece in the earth. He took no consideration of our thoughts, but instead when He sees us, sees that He created the best possible YOU that can exist.

The second stage is called the Larva or Caterpillar Stage. This is the place where the egg transforms into an insect that finds itself traveling by foot to get everywhere it desires to go. Whether on a sidewalk or in a tree, the caterpillar roams around waiting for that destined moment that he gets to finally become what looks impossible from around level In this place, to the naked eye, there is no way in the world that it will ever do anything but crawl, but those who doubt its ability are in for a surprise.

Growing up in our teenage years I recall those more "seasoned" than us, encouraging us to take our time. Like any other teenager ready to take over the world, over half of us didn't listen and found ourselves *going through* things we shouldn't have. This was the stage where we thought that we were grown and no one, not even those older than us, could tell us that they knew more than we did. This became that awkward stage – you know the one where you want to be an adult, but you have no desire to be held accountable with all of the things required to truly be one. It is also here, that one finds themselves in the "identity crisis," as we tried to discover who we were in the midst of bullies, cliques, haters, not being "enough" and so many other influences. My heart aches for the youth of today, as they face a depth of identity crisis that my generation many have never been able to survive. In this world, if you aren't popular or have the glitter and the gold, you are often underestimated. From the playhouse to the church house, people are often judged by their outer wealth versus their limitless possibilities, leaving

27

everyone from the youngest to the most advanced, always seeking, always looking, and often doubting and doing it all from the ground.

All of this brings us to stage 3, the Pupa or Chrysalis.

A hard-protective covering of the pupa becomes the home of transformation for the caterpillar. It is also in this place that we find that this caterpillar, if it genuinely wants to become a butterfly, must become completely vulnerable. Earlier generations always taught that it was best to simply be strong and never vulnerable, for that was an indicator of weakness. Trying to be a hard, many of us found ourselves trying to play the part of the "tough person" only to realize that we were just trying to cover our own insecurities. Just like the caterpillar, in this stage not only must we be willing to be vulnerable, but completely transparent as well. Yes, you heard that right – as the caterpillar prepares to become more than anyone expected, its physical body becomes completely broken down in the pupa, to the point where it becomes completely transparent. This process is required, as its body brings itself back together again, in preparation for maturity and taking flight. So here we are, in the ugly stage, wanting to belong but not knowing where you fit.

Too tall.

Too short.

Too fat.

Too thin.

Just. Too. Much.

This adventure brings us to stage four, Adulting. He knows us, who we are, and who we can become. Everything that He created He said, "It is Good!"

Once the caterpillar surrenders to the process and embraces their new body, it is now time to take flight. Like the butterfly, taking on the different stages helps us to see that God is in control of everything. He knows our beginning and end. Being a victim says to God that He messed up, not realizing that at some point we have to take responsibility for our own deliverance. It is important to note here, that when it is time for the butterfly to be released into their new world, they are required to flap their wings, or in layman's terms, fight their way out of the place of processing. As they flap their wings, every bit of residue is removed, enabling them to fly without sabotage or additional weight. If the butterfly is "helped" out of their cocoon or refuses to flap its way out, it only positions itself to die before they even get a chance to live! Stop staying in the egg, caterpillar, and chrysalis stages, not allowing God to bring you to that stage of completion. Become the butterfly that He intended you to be. Don't allow yourself to get stuck in the victim stage and become the beautiful butterfly you were meant to be.

Don't be a Victim! Be a Victor!

Transformation can be beautiful yet challenging. Share a moment where you were in the midst of a transformation. What happened? How did you feel? What did you learn In the process?

_____

_____

_____

_____

_____

_____

_____

_____

_____

_____

_____

_____

_____

_____

_____

_____

_____

_____

_____

_____

_____

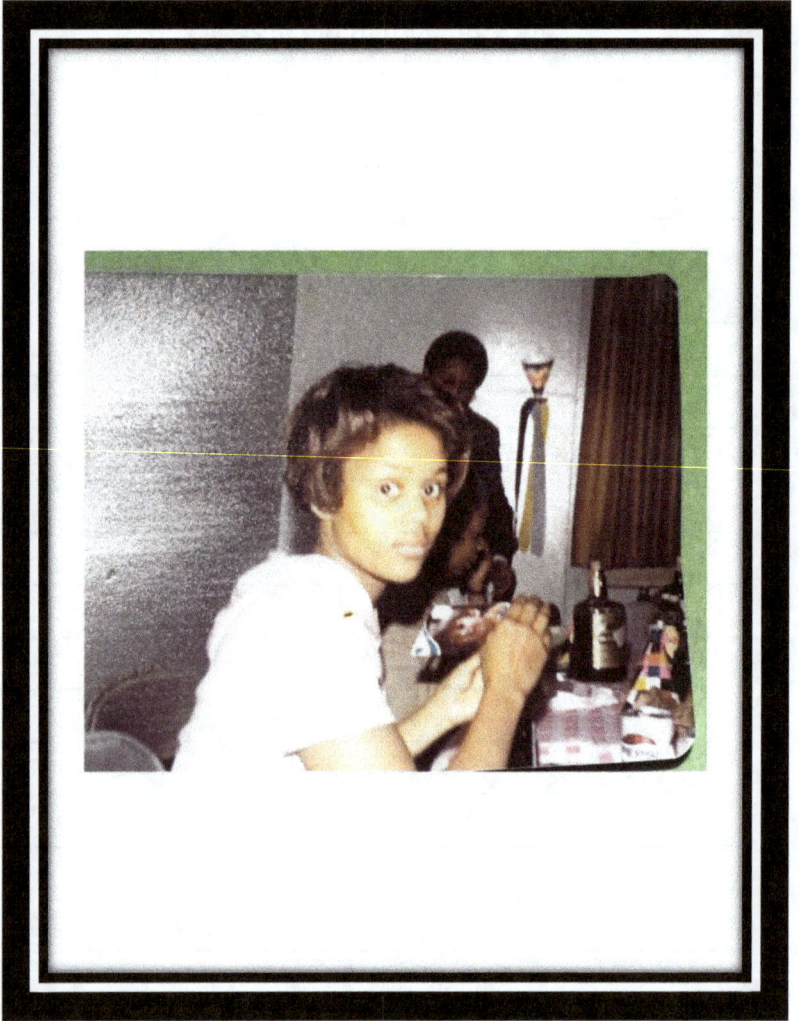

Chapter 2:

The Relationship of Martha and Mary

Martha was so hospitable! She was little Miss Homemaker. She believed in Jesus. She wanted everything to be exactly right. Excellence was her focus- there is no way that could have been the wrong approach, right? How many of us have taken on the Martha spirit, working so diligently in the church? Every time the doors are open, we are there. Day after day we can be found busy doing everything, but what God wants us to do. Martha is the one who can almost come off as borderline disrespectful, but feels that because of her sacrifice, she has earned the ability of a free-spirited approach. How many times, have believers forgotten that it is unto God that we serve and have taken on a "less than servant-like" approach to their movements and motives?

Then, we have Mary. Mary understood that it was more important to get to know Jesus. Mary learned when to listen and when to work. Her humility was priceless, and she held nothing back when it came to her relationship with Jesus. Her posture is evident, as it is a pure reflection of her heart towards the Master. There's a difference in knowing about

God and knowing God. God wants our obedience not just our service. It's a heart matter.

[40] But Martha was very busy _and_ distracted with all of her serving responsibilities; and she approached Him and said, "Lord, is it of no concern to You that my sister has left me to do the serving alone? Tell her to help me _and_ do her part."

Luke 10:40

[12] When she poured this perfume on My body, she did it to prepare Me for burial. [13] I assure you _and_ most solemnly say to you, wherever this gospel [of salvation] is preached in the whole world, what this woman has done will also be told in memory of her [for her act of love and devotion]."

Matthew 26: 12-13

I grew up in the church and attended Sunday School, Bible Study, Morning worship faithfully. I guess you could say that I was on a "fast-track" - I sang in the choir and directed the choirs (all of them)! I got baptized at an early age at McLeansville First Baptist Church. I knew about Christ, but the true transformation had not taken place. My rebirth came on May 23, 1976. This was the day that I surrendered all to Jesus Christ and transformed from Martha, simply knowing about Him, to Mary, pursuing relationship WITH Him. This new belief became my fuel and my push and catapulted me right into destiny.

Growing up, I felt like I was always in someone else's shadow. I was always being compared to someone else. When I wanted to be myself, I was told I was being rebellious or different. There were times that it seemed easier to just break and become whoever the world wanted me to be, but my spirit knew better. Regardless of their opinion, I knew that different was good! Jesus was different! He didn't fit in anyone else's mold of who HE was supposed to be, and I had countless verses of scripture to prove that very point. He knew who He was and what His purpose was on the earth. Even as a youth, He would be found in the most unusual places and even into adulthood, was found using the unusual methods of healing, so much so, that His approach drew constant crowds in the thousands! My Father is creative, He's different, and I had no problem accepting that truth even the more as I saw the depth of His difference live in me!

Let's be honest – Even as adults, we work so hard trying to be like other people, not knowing the shoes those people had to walk in. We always hear of the peer pressure that children endure, while ignoring the same identity crisis that many adults live with day to day. From trying to be in a certain clique of people, to making sure our decisions please other people, we are constantly surrounded with simply trying to fit, somewhere. There is a saying that goes like this:

If you claim that you want someone else's anointing, be ready to go through what they went through to get it.

Why can't we be who God wants us to be? Why does it seem that it is so much easier to hear the voices of doubt instead of the voices of faith? If He wanted us to be alike, He would've had mass produced us. How boring would this world be then? We are all uniquely different, but we all carry His DNA. The worst thing we can do is try to become a duplicate of someone else. Instead, we are to be like Jesus, the perfect sacrifice ever given. What a privilege! What an honor!

[6] I am convinced *and* confident of this very thing, that He who has begun a good work in you will [continue to] perfect *and* complete it until the day of Christ Jesus [the time of His return].

Philippians 1:3-6

I am coming into being who God wanted me to be without a fight. I am a mother, grandmother, minister, teacher, and worshipper. Even until this very moment, I am yet becoming who God created. With every experience I have had and even come to endure now, I am faced with the opportunity to embrace and grow. For every trial and tribulation, I am being blessed beyond measure. I wasted so much time trying to be someone else, but there came a moment, and this may be the one for you where we all say, NO MORE.

Even as you embrace this newfound freedom, I pray that the following scriptures will help to inspire and push you.

[45] When they did not find Him, they went back to Jerusalem looking for Him [everywhere]. [46] Three days later they found Him in the [court of the] temple, sitting among the teachers, both listening to them and asking them questions. [47] All who heard Him were amazed by His intelligence *and* His understanding and His answers. [48] When they saw Him, they were overwhelmed; and His mother said to Him, "Son, why have You treated us like this? Listen, Your [k]father and I have been [greatly distressed and] anxiously looking for You." [49] And He answered, "Why did you have to look

for Me? Did you not know that I had to be [i]in My Father's *house*?"

Luke 2:45-49

[13] For You formed my innermost parts; You knit me [together] in my mother's womb. [14] I will give thanks *and* praise to You, for I am fearfully and wonderfully made; Wonderful are Your works, And my soul knows it very well.

Psalm 139:13-14

[12] I assure you *and* most solemnly say to you, anyone who believes in Me [as Savior] will also do the things that I do; and he will do even greater things than these [in extent and outreach], because I am going to the Father.

John 14:12

As we close out this chapter on Martha and Mary, it is important to note the competition and comparison that exists. Have you ever found yourself in this place of comparison either by your words or the words of others? Share your thoughts here.

_____

_____

_____

_____

_____

_____

_____

_____

_____

_____

_____

_____

_____

_____

_____

_____

_____

Chapter 3:

Hungry, Thirsty, Desperate: The Woman at the Well

Having five husbands to me is a lot. I had one husband for forty-two and a half years and to think about going through life with five, wow, I don't even want to think about it. This woman kept looking for love in all the wrong places. She searched high and low, embraced man after man, only to find herself empty and still seeking. I can only imagine her dating, falling in love and getting married, only to realize that the promise she thought she had finally secured was only a figment of her imagination all over again, leaving her embarrassed, hurt, and borderline helpless. Can you imagine finally getting a covering, only to go right back to barely surviving? What she needed, though she did not realize it in that moment, was the love of God. She needed salvation.

As I begin to date, there were a few men that I really cared about. I had made a promise that I would remain a virgin until marriage. I knew that once I made that promise to God, breaking it was not an option. My choice was quite unpopular, but at that time, I refused to break my Savior's heart. I realized that not only was I preserving one of the most important gifts I that I would ever give my Husband, but I was also shielding myself from unnecessary struggle and

41

warfare. My intent was strong, my conviction was too, but time matriculated and as a result, I had to fight and press into my freedom.

When we give ourselves to other men and women that God has not ordained for us to be with, we take on soul ties. What are soul ties? [1]One definition says this: "A soul tie, sometimes referred to as an emotional or spiritual cording, is an inexplicable, powerful, emotional bond to another person." It can be a deep emotional bond formed after intimacy but can also be a spiritual connection between two people. This "relationship" can transcend from a physical interaction or a "heart bond," causing one to take on the emotions, weight and even characteristics of another person. There are ungodly soul ties, sexual soul ties, mutual soul ties, etc., all of which have the ability to not only import that person to you, but other people that they have existing soul ties with as well. There are five types of soul ties:

Biological:

Formed through the means of physical intimacy. This soul tie also holds the potential for someone to take on attributes that their other "soul tie(s)" has/have formed other bonds with.

---

[1] Dr. Carla Marie Manly, "Date Smart"

Social:

Created by friendships and relationships through conversations, common interests, life circumstances, etc.

Emotional:

Incorporates the feelings, emotions, and weight of another person.

Spiritual:

The ability to take on the attributes of another person or persons.

Physical:

The adoption of attitudes and movements of another individual.

I only have one husband and that is the man God gave me. At an early age, God told him that I would be his wife, but I didn't agree. Years following, I was out doing my own thing, and unbeknownst to me, the men I was with were not my husband. As a result, I took on the soul ties of these men that did not belong to me. I took on the thought that I was only hurting myself when I slept (had sex) with these men. In that moment, I could not see my actions affecting anyone more than it affected me, but I did so much more than hurt myself — my movements leaked into hurting others around me, too. In those moments we do not acknowledge it, but it is through these spiritual bondages that we take on the spirits of those men. Our spirit man knows that something else has come in, trying to take over its space. Those spirits come in war with one another causing us to take on things we should not accept or possess. This can lead to us acting completely out of character, taking on attitudes, dispositions, reactions and even leave us fighting for and with people who do not even deserve our swing. At first, we may not realize or even see it, but time will always tell. As time progresses, eventually we connect all of the dots and realize that who we have become is not a result of a curse, but a result of our own decision. It is during these times that we feel like we deserve what we got. This place can leave us feeling hurt, broken, and yes, condemned, unless we make a decision to heal and get up from that place.

Some men will make you feel like they are the best thing since sliced bread. They will say whatever they have to just to get what they desire. As women, we begin to believe it and begin to develop low self-esteem because we have readjusted our mind to receive all of our affirmations, or lack thereof from them. Then, if we are not careful, we allow them to do and say any and everything they want to say to us. The sadness of this cycle is that the moment they take away what they said or go silent, the woman can find herself immediately going into a self-rejection phase, taking on the belief that he now holds the cards to who she is and what she is purposed to do.

The devil is a liar! Is there anything too hard for God?

No, I am who God says that I am!

Is it easy to get to that point? This depends on who we are before we consent to this place. Regardless of the decision, there anything too hard for God? Absolutely not! Even if this is your trial in this moment, the Father still seeks a relationship with you! I admonish you to ask Him to be the center of your life. Despite any place that you have been, God has the ability to cleanse you, restore you and develop you into the one He purposed for you to be!

2 [looking away from all that will distract us and] focusing our eyes on Jesus, who is the Author and Perfecter of faith [the first incentive for our belief and the One who brings our faith to maturity], who for the joy [of accomplishing the goal] set before Him endured the cross, [b]disregarding the shame, and sat down at the right hand of the throne of God [revealing His deity, His authority, and the completion of His work].

Hebrews 12:2

Take this moment and these next two pages to think about any soul ties that are in your life. Remember, this can be biological, social, emotional, spiritual or physical. Who are they? What happened? Why have they been permitted to stay connected to you?

_____

_____

_____

_____

_____

_____

_____

_____

_____

_____

_____

_____

_____

_____

_____

_____

Chapter 4:

Joseph's Destiny Interwoven

34 Opening his mouth, Peter said:

"Most certainly I understand now that God is not one to show partiality [to people as though Gentiles were excluded from God's blessing], 35 but in every nation the person who fears God and does what is right [by seeking Him] is acceptable *and* welcomed by Him.

Acts 10:34-35

Can a woman have characteristics of a man? Contrary to the world's belief, of course she can! God is no respecter of person. Joseph rose in power from a slave to ruler of Egypt. He was casted away by his family, the lie was released to his father that he was dead by his own brothers, he ended up in jail and even found himself being forgotten! Regardless of his process and his journey, he possessed an anointing that could not be duplicated and went from being in jail to in demand!

Was I ever a slave? Yes, a slave to the sins of this world. Have I become a ruler? Of course, because I am a Queen. I am known for my personal integrity and a woman of spiritual sensitivity. What matters in life is not so much about the events or circumstances, but it is how we respond to them; with God's help, any situation can be used for good.

38 So Pharaoh said to his servants, "Can we find a man like this [a man equal to Joseph], in whom is the divine spirit [of God]?"

Genesis 41:38

Being from a large family has advantages and disadvantages. I was considered the middle child. I always felt like the black sheep of the family. Out of eight children, I was chosen to be uprooted from my family to live with another relative. Needless to say, I was left feeling abandoned and alone. It does not matter how saved or chosen a person is, we are never eliminated from at least one second in our lives when we ask the question,

What is wrong with ME?

I can only think of how Joseph felt. I can only think about how confused he must have been. A special coat from his father along with dreams and visions that were constantly misinterpreted as a takeover instead of provision for a later time of need even by the one who seemed to believe in him the most — I can only imagine! I wonder how many times Joseph was ready to simply give up and give in. How many days did he spend in anguish for simply being misunderstood? Based on history, to Joseph it would probably seem that if no one else believed in him, his father would. Joseph was the reminder that even in his father's old age, he still had the ability to produce! So, here Joseph stood, the miracle child of sorts, and despite the miracle he is, finds himself, alone.

We take on the victim mindset so easily. Sadly, the mentality has us looking for the first thing to give up to simply make it all better, to release the weight, which often includes God.

Why me?

Why not me?

[20] Now then, come and let us kill him and throw him into one of the [s]pits (cisterns, underground water storage); then we will say [to our father], 'A wild animal killed *and* devoured him'; and we shall see what will become of his dreams!"

Genesis 37:20

Joseph ended up being thrown in a cistern – a place meant to hold water. In other words, Joseph was thrown into a place that was not completing its purpose, hoping that Joseph would not be able to complete his either! Had Joseph fought against his brother's, he would not have gotten the blessing God had waiting on him. Had Joseph retaliated and sought revenge, he could have sabotaged his own dream of one day being a key vessel who would help ensure the livelihood of his family. As crazy as this may sound, it is indeed the truth – it was through this level of attack that Joseph found himself being thrusted into a journey that otherwise, he may have never taken. Think about it,

Would he have ever realized how much he could survive?

Would he have ever realized how valuable he was?

Would he have ever met Pharoah?

So many questions to answer and so many victories in the balance! As I reflect back on my experience, I was angry at first, but soon grew to know that it was a blessing instead. I cannot describe the feeling of being the only one relocated, and the only one pulled away from everyone else. We do not always know why God is taking us the route we are on, but we must trust God enough to know that He has our best interest in mind no matter how heavy the weight. At times, did

I feel that it was too much? Yes! Did I ever find myself doubting ME? Of course! Despite the voices in my head, I had to make a decision to focus on the voice of God!

¹³ No temptation [regardless of its source] has overtaken *or* enticed you that is not common to human experience [nor is any temptation unusual or beyond human resistance]; but God is faithful [to His word—He is compassionate and trustworthy], and He will not let you be tempted beyond your ability [to resist], but along with the temptation He [has in the past and is now and] will [always] provide the way out as well, so that you will be able to endure it [without yielding, and will overcome temptation with joy].

1 Corinthians 10:13

In my mind, I had to be missing something, but in this case the only thing I was missing was the revelation of how big of a blessing this was for me. He worked it out for my good even when I did not understand. I am so glad I let go of the victim mentality. It's so easy to get caught up in the victim mold but being a victor is so much greater.

²⁸ And we know [with great confidence] that God [who is deeply concerned about us] causes all things to work together [as a plan] for good for those who love God, to those who are called according to His plan *and* purpose.

Romans 8:28

Have you ever been faced with rejection, whether by family, friends, or more importantly, self? What happened? How did you recover?

_____

_____

_____

_____

_____

_____

_____

_____

_____

_____

_____

_____

_____

_____

_____

_____

_____

_____

_____

_____

Chapter 5:

The Beauty of Esther

Throughout our lives, we have heard, read, or seen something that we felt had happened before. Life can be even a turn of events, a challenge or even a short fairy tale. Thus, begin the life that I have lived.

16 "Go, gather all the Jews that are present in Susa, and observe a fast for me; do not eat or drink for three days, night or day. I and my maids also will fast in the same way. Then I will go in to [see] the king [without being summoned], which is against the law; and if I perish, I perish."

Esther 4:16

Let's start with Esther. Her beauty and character won the heart of a King. She was an orphan who lived with her uncle and was also raised by her cousin, Mordecai. Despite loss, she was raised to be courageous, open for advice and willing to act when the time was right. Based on her beauty, Esther could have been misjudged. Imagine how we look at people today - oftentimes, we look and assume that because a person is extremely handsome or beautiful, they are stuck up, anti-social, mean, and unfriendly but that was not Esther at all. She was always more concerned and caring about others over her own security.

If we dig deeper into her life, we also find out that not only did her beauty reward her with a seat as the new Queen, but later even saved the life of King Xerxes as her cousin uncovered a conspiracy to save his life. She was willing to use her voice and influence to establish victory in the kingdom and in the land at her own expense, without fear, and without regret.

At the age of seven, I stood before my king. What did he see in me? I saw a skinny little girl with funny looking eyes and three ponytails, but God was showing him more than my natural eyes could see. He did not see the little girl He saw in the mirror - he saw his queen! Me not knowing what the future held for either of us caused me to disregard the entire possibility of our future, but there was my king, trusting God to lead, guide, and direct our paths. To this day I thank God for giving us the faith, courage, and strength to move forward in Him. We can try to travel this journey on our own; it may go well for a while but having God on our side is the best decision that we can ever make and will let us see, that through Him, we can do all things.

13 I can do all things [which He has called me to do] through Him who strengthens *and* empowers me

[to fulfill His purpose—I am self-sufficient in Christ's sufficiency; I am ready for anything and equal to anything through Him who infuses me with inner strength and confident peace.]

Philippians 4:13

When you are stuck in the traditions, afraid to move or do anything different, fear can get a good grip on you. We can find ourselves saying everything from "it can't be true," to "it can't possibly be for us!" Even before truly accepting the man of God that He was blessing me with, I found myself with the same doubts and fears, looking for every reason why NOT, but God ordained us! What did I learn from that place in my life? We have to believe that God's Word is true. I had to forget about myself, my doubts and concerns and simply follow God. We can do it God's way or our way but doing it our way often leads to a long and often unnecessary road. The truth is, that what God wants will often require a major shift from us. This shifting requires us to ignore every potential obstacle and relentlessly press into our purposed destiny. I do not want to be the bearer of bad news, but this change will not be easy or comfortable, but it is indeed necessary.

We can choose to go the short route (God's way) or the long route like the children of Israel. It has been said and proven, that the land of Canaan was only five to seven days away, but yet it took the Israelites forty years to obtain it. Along the way, many had to fall off, especially those who did not believe or simply wanted it their way. Take a moment and imagine walking in circles for that long. Imagine what it must have eventually smelled like, as people were lost on this journey and what became a walk in the wood eventually became a cemetery for those who would never get to see the promise! If we are not careful, we will allow our own will to disrupt the manifestation of what God has for us! Obedience is better than sacrifice. I chose to step out of tradition and follow God! It is clear to me, now more than ever, that where God is taking me will allow me to move out of the way even the more and allow Him to move me in the right path.

Staying in tradition can cause you to feel like a victim.

I chose to be a Victor.

Despite every victim opportunity, you have been endowed with POWER and INFLUENCE! Share one time when these two entities have shown up for YOU! No victory is too small! Ready? Set? GO!

_____

_____

_____

_____

_____

_____

_____

_____

_____

_____

_____

_____

_____

_____

_____

_____

_____

_____

_____

_____

_____

Chapter 6:

The Accusation of Bathsheba

Bathsheba was a beautiful woman. She was attending to her own business. Unknowing to her, she was being watched. The chain of events in our life, rather willing or unwilling, cause consequences. We may feel that it is just a little sin, but this is an underestimated thought. Sin is Sin. There is no little or big sin. Regardless of the size or the origin they all have the capacity to break God's heart. Sin has the capacity to lead us into unfathomed experiences and unimaginable consequences. When we allow sin to take hold in our lives, we must be ready for those consequences.

26 When Uriah's wife [Bathsheba] heard that her husband Uriah was dead, she mourned for her husband. 27 And when the time of mourning was past, David sent *word* and had her brought to his house, and she became his wife and bore him a son. But the thing that David had done [with Bathsheba] was evil in the sight of the LORD.

II Samuel 11:26-27

My life has been a roller coaster ride. So many ups and downs. If we always had ups, we would not feel that we needed Jesus, for it is in the down times that we seek God for the strength to get through. It is truly through the trials of our lives that we realize just how strong we really are and just how dedicated God's Word really is concerning us.

Being molested by family and friends (so I thought), was one of the more horrific things that I ever experienced; being told as the victim, I warranted it because I was so fast and that the reason it happened was probably the second. I allowed it to define who and what I was put on this earth for. There I was, no longer holding on to my innocence but instead having it ripped away without my agreement and without my desire. The more people talked, the more I put on. I could have followed in that path and took on the label and scars that were put on me but even then, I decided to change my mind. Thanks be to God that His still small voice began to speak to me to tell me who and Who's I was.

Why are we so quick to believe what people say about us and not what God says?

Why are we so dedicated to the doubt instead of the destiny?

Why do we find ourselves speaking loud about the disbelief and get quiet when victory shows up?

Having anyone put their hands on you in an inappropriate way, be it through touch or intercourse without your consent, is wrong in every way. Being told that "it is okay" to fall victim to such behavior by people you thought had your best interest in mind or having you to believe that it's all you and not them is demonic. Being made to be the aggressor or for one to say that it happened because you asked for it, is not the truth at all - it happened because they took it from you. Being made to think that I caused what happened to me were the words that echoed in my ears.

Statistics say, that 87% of our thoughts are negative, therefore, we must make a decision to maximize the 13% that remains! Why do we allow ourselves to believe man over God, the negative over the positive? For years I did, "but God!" He picked me up from the thoughts I had in my head and put a psalm in my heart to show me that I was fearfully and wonderfully made; marvelous are thy works. No matter what is said to you, about you. God did not make junk!

This is your AFFIRMATION STATION! Use this space to speak well of yourself! Use this space to ENCOURAGE yourself! Use this space to declare your win!

_____

_____

_____

_____

_____

_____

_____

_____

_____

_____

_____

_____

_____

_____

_____

_____

_____

_____

Chapter 7:

Racheal & Leah: The Sibling Rivalry

The tale of two sisters. Here, we have Leah, the oldest of the two. She was given in marriage to a man that loved her sister by way of trickery. Her father, Laban, advised Jacob, who was deeply in love with Rachel, that in order to obtain her, he would have to work for him for seven years. At the end of this time, instead of Laban giving away Rachel, he gave Jacob Leah instead. Once Jacob realized what had taken place, he was devastated but offered a "plan of restitution" from his new father-in-law. I feel a little sibling rivalry brewing up right here.

²⁵ And in the morning, behold, it was Leah! And Jacob said to Laban, "What is this you have done to me? Did I not serve with you for Rachel? Why then have you deceived me?" ²⁶ Laban said, "It is not so done in our country, to give the younger before the firstborn. ²⁷ Complete the week of this one, and we will give you the other also in return for serving me another seven years." ²⁸ Jacob did so and completed her week. Then Laban gave him his

daughter Rachel to be his wife. ²⁹ (Laban gave his female servant Bilhah to his daughter Rachel to be her servant.) ³⁰ So Jacob went into Rachel also, and he loved Rachel more than Leah, and served Laban for another seven years.

Genesis 29:25-29

Leah envied her sister because Leah's husband was in love with Rachel. She knew that she could not change her husband's affections for her sister but had something that her sister did not have — the ability to reproduce. She used her ability to bear children to get back at her sister every chance she got. You see, Rachel waited patiently for the day that she would marry the love of her life, only to find out that she couldn't give him children. It is later stated that the Lord saw that Leah was hated and therefore, opened up her womb to conceive. It was by this ability, that Leah birthed four sons, each believing that by her having them, Jacob's attention would be steered back towards her, not for the ability to continue the bloodline but for the chance at authentic love. We can allow the wrong motive towards someone to keep us from real joy.

³¹ When the LORD saw that Leah was hated, he opened her womb, but Rachel was barren. ³² And Leah conceived

and bore a son, and she called his name Reuben,[c] for she said, "Because the LORD has looked upon my affliction; for now my husband will love me." [33] She conceived again and bore a son, and said, "Because the LORD has heard that I am hated, he has given me this son also." And she called his name Simeon.[d] [34] Again she conceived and bore a son, and said, "Now this time my husband will be attached to me, because I have borne him three sons." Therefore his name was called Levi.[e] [35] And she conceived again and bore a son, and said, "This time I will praise the LORD." Therefore she called his name Judah.[f] Then she ceased bearing.

Genesis 29: 31-35

God has a way of turning our evil into His good. Rachel was once barren, but God opened up her womb, and she gave birth to two children.

Having a loving husband that cares, looks out for you, a husband that respects and adores you even with all your faults is one of the most priceless gifts that a woman can receive. God can bless us with a Husband who will give us the world if he could, but this outward blessing does not always reflect and inner transformation. We can be beautiful on the outside but have a Leah spirit (envy, jealousy) on the inside, feeling like you're never good enough, second hand, and always chosen last. This was my life and for a time, was my only expectation. When others would perform in front of friends, they were cute and applauded, but when I performed, I was told I was fast and too grown. As a result of responses and their words, I began to give up on myself and life. These words echoed in my spirit constantly and ultimately drowned out anything that God was trying to establish and re-enforce in me. This belief system can cause you to take on the negative instead of the positive and before you know it, you have given up the power and the Word God invested in you. Do not allow this to become you! You have the power in you to stop every voice and attempt of the enemy to strip you of life and life more abundantly.

¹⁰ The thief comes only to steal and kill and destroy. I came that they may have life and have it abundantly.

John 10:10

Loving life and yourself can take you so much further in life. As I reflect on the mirror I spoke about earlier, it was my Husband who saw the queen in me, but there came a day when I had to receive the queen, he, and even the more, God, saw in me!

You are worth more than crumbs!

You have a right to declare what you want!

You do not have to simply "accept" whatever is given to you!

There is more for you beyond this!

People have said, that "having a half of a man in my life is better than not having a man at all." If you have ever spoken this out of your mouth, even anything vaguely close, you have just taken on the victim mindset. Now don't get me wrong, Leah had her flaws, but she did not allow them to become her life. Despite the inner battles she fought constantly, she knew that she was made in God's image and everything that God made, He said "It is Good."

HELLO VICTOR! Yes, it's time to CROSSOVER! As you take this moment, BREATHE and prepare for the WIN! Take this moment and this space to say goodbye to the victim mentality. It's time to eulogize the past and prepare for the VICTORY ahead!

_____

_____

_____

_____

_____

_____

_____

_____

_____

_____

_____

_____

_____

_____

_____

_____

_____

_____

Chapter 8:

The Necessity of Mary, Martha, and Lazarus

20 **So when Martha heard that Jesus was coming, she went to meet Him, while Mary remained sitting in the house. 21 Then Martha said to Jesus, "Lord, if You had been here, my brother would not have died.**

John 11:20-21

Earlier in the book we talked about Mary and Martha. Now, I want to talk about their brother, Lazarus. Lazarus was a friend of Jesus. What a friend we have in Jesus! When we surrender our all to Jesus, our lives no longer belong to us, but to Him. God has ownership of our lives. We can't predict what He will do with it; this is part of the agreement of giving our lives over to Him.

The events surrounding Lazarus' sickness and death was to glorify God. Some may have looked at it, much like Martha, who questioned Jesus, in a way, concerning why He did not show up sooner. It seemed that if God was really going to be glorified, that Jesus would have shown up at the onset of the news of the illness of his friend, not after he was already dead, wrapped and "buried." It was here that Jesus not only heard of the news of Lazarus but waited before coming to perform the miracle of Lazarus' resurrection.

4 When Jesus heard this, He said, "This sickness will not end in death; but [on the contrary it is] for the glory *and* honor of God, so that the Son of God may be glorified by it."

John 11:4

Let's talk about a dead situation. Growing up, I made God a promise to remain a virgin, but because of life's twists and turns and low self-esteem, I went opposite of my promise. Upon getting married, my husband and I wanted to have children. For two years, we tried only to be told "no" time and time again. Looking to God, I got upset and told Him (as if He didn't know),

"I waited until marriage to get pregnant, so why haven't You allowed me to get pregnant. There are women out here getting rid of babies because they wanted the pleasure of sex but not the responsibility that come from unprotected sex. Why God? What have we done that You haven't allowed us to get pregnant?"

Who was I to even question God like that? It later became clear to me that I was taking on that victim mindset again. God began to speak to me in a dream - He told me it was my past sins that brought me to this point. People, when you think you've gotten away with sin, God will let you know. I was told by a family member of a doctor that was exceptionally good in **his** field. (God directed **her** to me.) Long story short, after one visit, some tests, and ten months later, I gave birth to my first daughter.

When we think a situation is dead, we must give it to God and allow Him to be the final word. We have to resolve that God has resurrection power and is able to do just what He said! Are you ready for this next statement? We have to make sure that we are not trying to hold God in a box.

²⁴ Martha said to him, "I know that he will rise again in the resurrection on the last day." ²⁵ Jesus said to her, "I am the resurrection and the life.[d] Whoever believes in me, though he die, yet shall he live, ²⁶ and everyone who lives and believes in me shall never die. Do you believe this?"

²⁷ She said to him, "Yes, Lord; I believe that you are the Christ, the Son of God, who is coming into the world."

John 11: 24-27

This part in our process is pivotal, because if we are not open to how God is going to do "it" for us, we can easily miss God's hand and presence in it. If we are simply relishing in the knowledge of God with no pursuit of relationship with Him, we will simply continue to rely and predict His next move based on what we think we know about Him. It is here that we must remember that God is infinite, and that we will never have the mental capacity to fully take in every single part of who He is.

God is in what we are in and cares about us coming out!

I encourage you, stand on the promises of God! Choose to be the Victor and not the Victim. Throughout our lives, we have heard, read, or seen something that we felt had happened before. Life can be a turn of events, a challenge or even a short fairy tale. I can tell you in full transparency, that I have seen what some may call a cycle, others may call de ja vue and some may even call a glimpse or prophetic vision concerning my life more times than I can count. I am grateful that God would even entrust me with it all — that He would allow me to become the depth of who He has called me to be, thus, begins the life that I have lived.

Let's chat about posture! At the crossroads of being a victim or choosing to become a victor, were you Martha or Mary? What was your posture then? What is your posture now?

_____

_____

_____

_____

_____

_____

_____

_____

_____

_____

_____

_____

_____

_____

_____

_____

_____

_____

_____

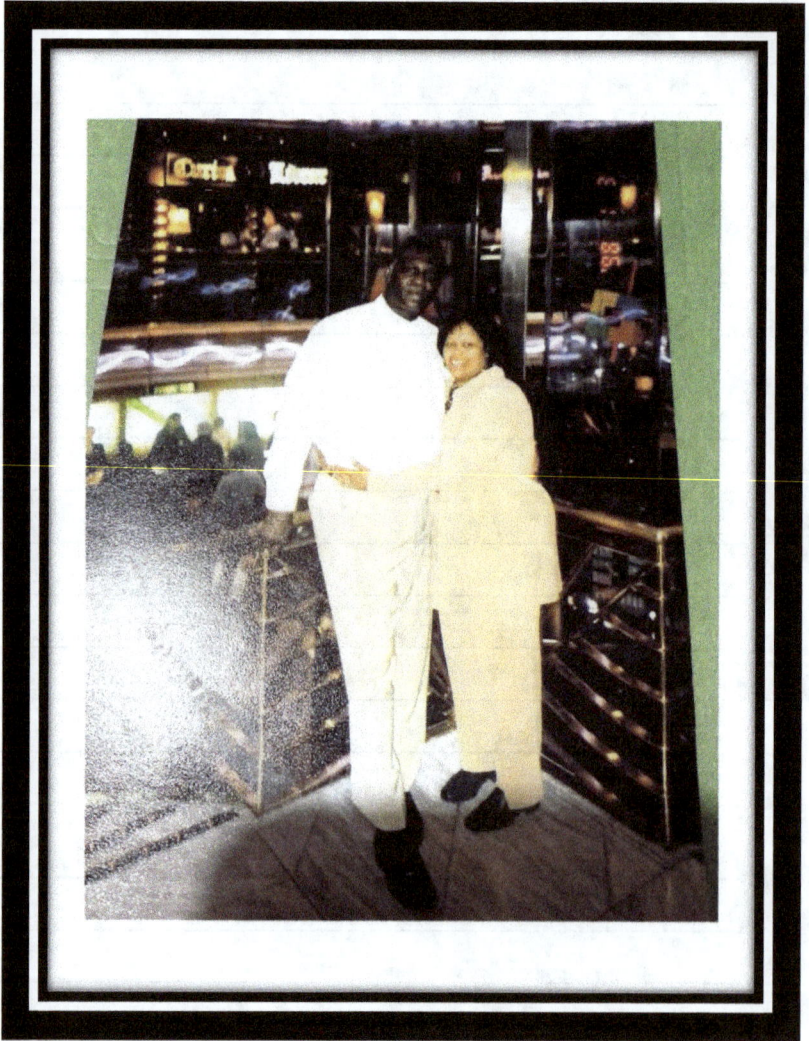

Chapter 9:

Queen Cynthia

I will never forget my path to finishing school. I began to think I was grown. I wanted my own place because I no longer wanted to abide by my mother's rule. To the outside world, I was talking like I had it altogether and had perfected my case. Despite my open defiance and desire to live independently, the enemy (inner me) had me believing that I was not good enough or had no one to love me. I was talking the talk and walking the walk but, honestly, I had low self-esteem. To my core, I felt that nothing I did was right, and that no one cared about me. If you would have asked me then, I would have told you that I felt as if I was just here to be used mostly by men. Maybe that was residue from the molestation, but at the time, that is how I truly felt. I had to snap out of that. That's the victim's mindset.

Who made me?

Who was I listening to?

God or man?

Over time, thank God, I recovered. I had to learn to trust the God I claimed that I believed in. I had to know without doubt or fear that God called me and made no mistake when He did. I had to accept the beauty that He created me in without question and fully resolve to serve Him regardless of my past but instead, pressing into the YES that I gave Him.

We make choices every day, rather to be good or bad, happy, or sad. Every day I had to learn to speak positive over myself. Again remember, shifting is not easy and it was not easy for me, however I knew that I had to let go of the victim mentality released over my life and accept my purpose, who patiently waited at the door of my heart waiting for me to open it. It was in this moment that I had to decide — Would I follow God or man? This decision is one of good versus evil, being a victim or a victor. This decision requires dedication, focus and letting go of anything or anyone who challenges it. This place requires relinquishing everything, the good, bad and the ugly to God, because He is fully aware of it anyway. This place requires the intimate and intentional decision to choose Christ over everything. This place requires you and I to rely on His voice, His leading, His reveal, as we press even the more into the beauty that awaits us. I chose Christ. Don't choose to go down the dark road of life but instead, choose the life of love, joy, peace, and happiness that is waiting for you. Will every day be great? No, but knowing who holds your day (Jesus Christ) will make each day better. Give Him your day. Give Him your life. This is the decision that saved mine. This is the decision that raised me up from a life of being a victim. Based on the world, I should have fallen for their estimations about me, but thanks be to God, He has positioned my life to prove every lie wrong.

In choosing Christ, I am no longer a victim.

In choosing Christ, I am victorious.

Author Cynthia Shaw

Cynthia Shaw has spent most of her life serving the Lord and others. She is a worshiper, author, minister and the recent founder and CEO of A Widow's Wisdom, a vision birthed after her husband of forty-two years went to meet Jesus.

Cynthia enjoys helping people! She has volunteered with numerous schools in her area, serves Thanksgiving and Christmas dinners to the homeless, and assists with various health fairs as well all throughout the year. She is undoubtedly a servant, a worshiper and a lover of people.

Cynthia loves the occasional pampering with manicures, pedicures, and massages. Her favorite pastime is creating new memories with family and friends, especially her ten grandchildren and one great granddaughter. There is a song that starts off with, "If I can help somebody," and these words remain to be her pursuit in her daily life and through every act of service.

Connect with Author Cynthia Shaw:

Email: authorcynthiashaw22@gmail.com

Phone: (336) 303-0878

www.ingramcontent.com/pod-product-compliance
Lightning Source LLC
LaVergne TN
LVHW022112080426
835511LV00007B/772